TOMM DALI

MOBILE MARKETING

The Ultimate Guide to Successful Mobile Marketing, Learn Insider Strategies and Best Practices on How to Tap Into The Always Growing Mobile Shopping Market

Descrierea CIP a Bibliotecii Naționale a României
TOMM DALI
   MOBILE MARKETING. The Ultimate Guide to Successful Mobile Marketing, Learn Insider Strategies and Best Practices on How to Tap Into The Always Growing Mobile Shopping Market / Tomm Dali – Bucharest: Editura My Ebook, 2020
   ISBN

TOMM DALI

MOBILE MARKETING

The Ultimate Guide to Successful Mobile Marketing, Learn Insider Strategies and Best Practices on How to Tap Into The Always Growing Mobile Shopping Market

My Ebook Publishing House
Bucharest, 2020

CONTENTS

INTRODUCTION

If you're looking to skyrocket sales, connect with your target audience, and send an **endless surge of highly-targeted traffic** to your website, you must tap into the **power of mobile marketing.**

The number of mobile shoppers is at an all-time high, and it'll only continue to grow over the next few years. With more people using their mobile devices to interact online, conduct business and complete purchases, it's crucial that you build a business that is both mobile- friendly, and engages the busy, on the go shopper.

In fact, according to Salesforce.com, **5 percent of all digital retail traffic** flows through social channels, such as Pinterest, Facebook and Instagram!

Consider what this could mean for your business. You could easily double, maybe even triple your sales just by tapping into the ever- growing market of mobile shoppers.

This special report reveals the insider strategies to creating high converting marketing campaigns on some of the leading social platforms so that you can get your message in front of thousands of potential customers.

I'll also show you how to join the ranks of successful ecommerce websites who have utilized apps in order to maximize sales and build brand loyalty faster and easier than they ever thought possible.

So, without further delay, let's get started!

CHAPTER 1

WHAT IS MOBILE MARKETING?

Let's start with a quick definition of exactly what mobile marketing is:

Quite simply, mobile marketing is the concept of developing marketing campaigns that appeal specifically to mobile device users.

This could include everything from the structure of your website, and how it allows mobile visitors to interact and connect with your products, but it also could comprise of ad campaigns that are primarily designed to attract mobile shoppers.

The future of mobile marketing is here, and if you're not working to implement some sort of mobile marketing strategy into your business, you're missing out on a massive segment of your market.

According to Marketing Land, **nearly 40% of Internet time** each day is spent on mobile devices, while **more than 70% browse** more web pages on tablets rather than smartphones.

And while a few years ago, most people would connect to social media sites using desktop computers or laptops, these days most users use the available apps, such as the one Facebook, Skype and Twitter.

The same goes for retail-based apps such as, Amazon and Ebay, just to name a few.

In the next chapter, we'll look at some of the ways people have been successful with mobile marketing campaigns and how you can follow their lead.

CHAPTER 2

MOBILE MARKETING STRATEGIES

There are many ways you can implement mobile marketing into your business strategy so that you're able to broaden your outreach and connect with a larger segment of your market.

Here are a few ways to get started:

QR Codes:

QR Codes are scanned by recipients using their smartphones. Once scanned, users are then directed to a specific website, landing page or offer. You can feature QR codes on business cards, flyers, in direct mail packages, or even postcards, just to give you a few ideas! Create your QR codes here: https://www.qrstuff.com/

Location-based marketing:

This is a direct marketing strategy in which specific ads appear based on a user's current location.

For example, restaurants can take advantage of location-based marketing by having their place of business featured whenever a potential patron is within a couple miles from their business.

In-app Marketing:

With services like *AdMob by Google*, you can easily promote your website's app inside of other popular apps to generate more brand awareness, increase clicks and maximize revenue.

Check it out here:

https://www.google.com/admob/platform.html

In-game Marketing:

Have you ever played a game and suddenly an advertisement appears that you must watch before you can continue to play? This is in-game marketing, and it's one of the most effective ways to get your message in front of potential customers without having to spend a fortune in advertising. You can take a closer look by visiting in-game advertising agencies including: https://www.rapidfire.com/

SMS Marketing:

This strategy involves capturing a user's phone number so that you can send them text-based offers. According to Mitek, over 80% of Millennials revealed that their phone is the first thing they check each day, SMS marketing can be a very effective technique at getting attention and maximizing exposure.

In fact, compared to email campaigns that can sit in a users inbox for days (or worse, caught in a spam filter and never seen), with SMS, you're able to get your message seen almost immediately after they've been delivered.

In addition, with SMS marketing you're able to interact in a far more effective way by gaining valuable feedback from recipients as well as tracking response rates.

Here are a few SMS marketing platforms to consider:

https://www.slicktext.com/ https://www.eztexting.com
https://www.protexting.com

CHAPTER 3

CREATING AN APP FOR YOUR BUSINESS

According to Bizrate Insights, over 45% of all U.S. shoppers make purchases via the use of retail apps, at least once a month.

Think about how many apps you may personally use, such as EBay, Amazon, Walmart or Groupon. These companies utilize apps to encourage sales and build customer loyalty. Chances are, you've likely made at least one purchase using an app in the past few months.

And according to Criteo Inc, app-based shoppers are **three times more likely to make a purchase** after viewing a product detail page than even mobile web shoppers!

In the world of e-commerce, apps are certainly changing the landscape of online shopping.

One of the best ways to interact with on-the-go consumers is by offering them an app that makes it easy to browse and purchase your products.

Consider just how many people don't have the time to sit at the computer when evaluating products. If you want to boost sales and build a loyal customer base, you **need** to cater to the busy parent, the on-the-go professional, and the younger crowd of customers that spend hours of their day on mobile devices.

Here are a few more reasons why it's important to consider creating an app as a digital extension of your brand:

Apps Simplify the Purchasing Process

Once a person becomes comfortable using an app, chances are they'll continue to use it every time they purchase, or connect to your community or online store. Apps make shopping fast and easy, especially for those with limited time.

Apps Provide Invaluable Customer Data

Apps allow you to collect important customer data, including purchase histories, email addresses, as well as age and location demographics.

This information can be invaluable when creating ad campaigns or marketing initiatives, allowing you to better target your audience.

Reward Apps Build Loyalty

Consumers love a bargain and they also appreciate being rewarded for purchasing through your store. In fact, loyalty-based reward apps are so popular that customers will often remain with the brands that offer them reward incentives even when the prices of products are higher than competing companies that fail to offer an app!

Tip: Consider creating a loyalty based app that rewards users with special discounts and coupons as well as providing them with the ability to keep track of the rewards/points so they're encouraged to continue shopping with you.

This is one of the easiest ways to improve customer retention and build a trusted brand.

So how can you build an app for your e-commerce website in order to boost sales and satisfy the ever-growing demand from mobile shoppers?

Here are a few ways to get started:

Appy Pie:

With their ecommerce app builder, you can integrate your current product listing from your website right into your new ecommerce app so that customers can buy and sell from within the app. Engage with your customers through effective push notifications from App Builder Appy Pie, and keep them updated regarding new offers and products.

Visit: https://www.appypie.com/e-commerce-app-builder

Adiante Apps:

Create an e-commerce app quickly and easily even if you have zero experience building applications!

With Adiante Apps, you can:

1. Integrate your online shop

2. Send notifications about the newest offers and items added into your inventory

3. Create exclusive coupons

4. Guide with GPS your customers to your physical location

5. Show pictures and videos of your facilities

6. Create satisfaction surveys about your products

7. Integrate your social networks (twitter, facebook)

8. and many more things...

Visit:

https://www.adianteapps.com/info/make-your-online-shop- app

Top Recommended: Shopify

One of the easiest ways to build an app for your store is by combining the power of Shopify with the mobile app creator available here: https://apps.shopify.com/plobalapps-mobile-application and here: http://www.shoutem.com/app/e-commerce

Spend some time evaluating the different app development options in order to find the one that works best for you. Then create an app that encourages customer engagement and loyalty.

Here are a few other ways to develop your app:

Hire a Developer

You can easily hire an app developer from marketplaces like www.eLance.com and www.Freelancer.com. Just make sure that your developer is available for ongoing support and updates whenever needed.

Hire an Agency

If your budget allows for it, you could outsource your app to an agency who would be responsible for providing maintenance, updates, bug fixes and security protocols. Agencies can also work on developing future enhancements and personalization options which can add value to a customer's experience.

Here is a list of available agencies to help you get started: https://experts.shopify.com/developers

CHAPTER 4

SOCIAL MARKETING ON MOBILE

If you're looking to get your business in front of thousands of prospective customers, you'll want to consider creating targeted ads within the most popular social media platforms and communities.

Here's how to get started:

Instagram: http://www.Instagram.com

Boasting over **400 million users** each day, and over 100 million photos shared, Instagram is a titan in the realm of social marketing. One of the easiest ways to reach your audience is with Instagram ads.

Advertisers have several options to choose from including:

1. Video Ads
2. Photo Ads
3. Carousel Ads (
4. Stories Ads

Instagram ads uses Facebook's demographic data to display highly- targeted ads. This means it's exceptionally easy for you to reach a **very specific segment of your market**.

You'll also gain access to in-depth monitoring, tracking and historical data that provides you with the information you need to gauge the effectiveness of your ad campaigns.

Instagram's advertising model is based on **CPM** (cost per impressions) which means that you pay only when your ads are seen.

In addition, you can choose between a **daily budget** (where you cap your spending off per day once it reaches your limit), or set a **lifetime budget** where your ads expire only after the entirety of your budget has been exhausted.

Another way to gain followers and maximize exposure at absolutely no cost is to post content regularly, and use relevant hashtags. Hashtags are those things you see that look like:

#hashtag, and they are equivalent to keywords. You must use the # sign in front of the tag, and there must be no spaces.

If you have multiple words in your hashtag, you can either combine them all into one word like this:

#thisisyourhashtag

Or, you can separate them with underscores, like this:

#this_is_your_hashtag

You can have up to 30 hashtags in each Instagram post.

Yelp: http://www.Yelp.com

With over **90 million unique mobile users** every single month, you won't want to overlook the potential exposure that Yelp has to offer.

If you own a brick and mortar business, you'll want to set up a page on Yelp that allows for customers to post reviews and feedback.

You can further boost exposure with Yelp by paying for a sponsored advertisement.

Facebook Advertising:

One of the most popular ways to advertise to mobile users on Facebook is with their carousel format which gives advertisers the opportunity to feature multiple product images and links within one ad.

There are two different places you can create an ad on Facebook - the Ads Manager and the Power Editor. The Power Editor includes more features, but the Ads Manager is said to be a bit easier for people who are just starting out, however you can also use both in different ways.

For example, you could create your ads in the Power Editor, and then monitor your campaigns and make changes with the Ads Manager.

Fortunately, Facebook has a solid interface that walks you through the entire process.

>>

https://www.facebook.com/adsmanager/manage/campaigns

Facebook advertising is one of the platforms that provides the most targeted campaign options. With their sophisticated ad system you can target your ads based on gender, location, hobbies/interests, occupation, education, age, as well as many other options.

You can also choose where and when your ads appear which makes it a powerful advertising platform when trying to reach mobile shoppers as you can choose to show your ads only to mobile users and even specific mobile devices.

Creating a great ad can take some time, and you might have to test a few different ads before you find one that has the best CTR (click-thru ratio, or the number of people who see the ad and click on it vs. the number of people who don't.)

Facebook Pages

You can also use your Facebook business page to drive targeted traffic to your ecommerce store in a few different ways. To start, if you own a brick-and-mortar store, you should make sure you list your business hours and location in the About section of your page so that potential customers can easily find you. Also, those using Facebooks "Nearby in your neighborhood" feature will see your page.

A Facebook page provides your business with the opportunity to connect to customers, provide updates on specials, discounts or time- limited events. You could also run giveaways and contests on your page in order to boost exposure and drive fresh traffic to your online store.

You can create your Facebook business page here: https://www.facebook.com/business/learn/set-up-facebook-page

Create a Facebook store

If you're looking for a quick and easy way to set up a Facebook store, check out https://www.shoptab.net. They make it easy to create a Facebook shop within minutes and all stores are optimized for use with the Facebook app. Another solution is available at https://www.bigcommerce.ca/facebook/

Pinterest Advertising:

With Pinterest's Buyable Pins, merchants can sell their products directly to their mobile audience without forcing them to leave the platform.

After you've been approved, you can feature as many products as you wish while creating a frictionless checkout experience that makes it easy for mobile shoppers to purchase your products quickly, all from within the Pinterest app.

You'll need a Pinterest business account in order to utilize their Buyable Pins advertising platform and once you're ready, you can apply via Shopify at: https://www.shopify.com/pinterest or BigCommerce at https://www.bigcommerce.com/pinterest/

Tip: Review Pinterest's policies prior to requesting approval in order to determine if your business is eligible. You can find out more here: https://about.pinterest.com/commerce-policies

Here's how Buyable Pins work:

After you're approved, any pins on your public boards that link back to specific products will now feature an "Add to Bag" button. You can display your buyable pins in many places including within category feeds, search results, on boards of other people who have saved your products and within the home feed.

Once you have Buyable Pins enabled, you can take advantage of Pinterest's' extended advertising options which enable you to promote your Buyable Pins in order to maximize exposure. And with Pinterest's advertising channels you'll be able to easily monitor traffic and sales from within your Ads Manager.

CHAPTER 5

BEST PRACTICES FOR MOBILE DEVICES

The following list of best practices for mobile devices includes tips for both users and website developers. It is estimated that there will be 2 Billion Smartphone users by the year 2015. Note that this number does not include all the other types of mobile devices. This is a growing trend that should not be overlooked by anyone.

Ensure that you check your device for 3G or 4G capabilities before purchasing. Otherwise you will not be able to use the internet when out shopping or travelling. Understand that a Wi-Fi hotspot allows you to connect to the internet from any location.

1. Start using a responsive theme on your website.

2. Consider using SMS or text message marketing in your business.

3. Ensure that your site can be easily viewed on all mobile devices. Test it out.

4. Don't forget about incorporating social media sites as well.

5. Allow employees to use mobile devices as a way to stay connected.

6. Make use of mobile Applications.

7. Set strong passwords on your devices. Have them automatically lock aUer so many minutes of inactivity.

8. If you lose your device report it stolen quickly.

9. Use your mobile device to attend conferences and meetings.

10. Allow sales reps to use a mobile device when out on the road. A great way to stay connected to the office and to get question answered quickly.

11. Download Apps that make your life easier. Calendars, shopping lists and planners are all useful Apps.

12. Operating systems on mobile devices can be hacked so take precautions.

13. When designing your responsive website leave more white space on your pages.

14. Add more padding around images so they don't appear bunched up when viewed on a mobile device.

15. When setting up a text message campaign get permission and abide by the regulations.

16. Confirmation is sill required for SMS message, get documentation that proves this.

17. Don't send out false text messages, these will just land you in trouble.

18. Photos, audios, videos and presentations can all be sent via a text message.

19. Mobile marketing is going to be the wave of the future, so jump on the bandwagon now.

20. Set up a targeted campaign for mobile users, use things such as time of day and location to connect with them.

As you can see it is important for you to stay on top of this growing trend and to use it both personally and professionally.

CHAPTER 6

GAINING CUSTOMERS WITH MOBILE APPS

If you have an online website for your business, your customers are going to expect to connect to it, regardless of their location. This means that your site needs to be responsive. Having a responsive theme is one way to keep interacting with your customers. Of course, as a business owner, you also want to focus on attracting new customers and/or readers on a regular basis. One way to do this is by using mobile Apps.

There is no doubting that people love using their mobile devices, they spend hours each day staying connected to the internet and their friends and family. Mobile devices make it easy to perform tasks quickly. It is so much easier to send a text message to someone. Before this luxury existed, if you didn't have a mobile phone, you would have to find a pay phone.

A mobile App or Application is basically a simple piece of software. This software is installed on your mobile device and helps make a certain task easier to perform. An App normally shortens the steps in any type of procedure or function. Stores offer Apps so that you can speed up your purchase time. Weather Apps allow you to see your local forecast in seconds.

As a business owner you want to benefit from the popularity of mobile Apps. Just take a look at the line ups outside of stores when a new mobile device is launched! No wonder you want to take advantage of this trend.

You can hire a software developer to create a simple App for your business. Once you have it created you want to market it to your customers with vigor. There is no point in getting an App developed and then not marketing it. A good App can easily help you attract new customers, as well as extending the marketing reach of your business.

Remember to test your App to ensure that it is easy to use, loads quickly and adds a fun element. Plus take the : me to make sure that it works with all the top social media sites. This is a sure - fire way to give your App more exposure. People love to share things that they enjoy and getting your App shared across social media could potentially explode your business reach.

Don't forget to associate your branding with your App. Create a snazzy looking icon that will make it stand out. You may even want to give it away for free!

CHAPTER 7

MOBILE MARKETING FOR YOUR BUSINESS

If you run a business today, it is important to consider how mobile users are accessing your website. Have you actually checked to see if your current website is mobile responsive? If you haven't, it is something you should look into.

Creating a mobile version of your site is not that difficult. In fact, many newer WordPress themes come as a mobile responsive theme. It may even be worth your while to change your theme.

You should get into the habit of checking your Google Analytics or website statistics log. Check to see what browser people are accessing your site with. No doubt there will be a high number of mobile users. This number is sure to increase as the popularity of mobile devices grows.

When creating your website and adding new content it pays to consider how mobile users will see it. This is very true for ecommerce type sites. You want to ensure that your customers can buy via their mobile devices. Otherwise you may be losing out on sales.

You need to understand that people are so busy and even if they access a message on their smartphone, it doesn't mean that they will visit your site when they get home to their computer. Chances are they will get busy with something else and forget about your great offer, no matter how enticing it was.

Take the ?me to test out the purchase system on your mobile device. If you don't own one, then ask a friend to test a purchase for you. Things to take notice of include how the website itself displays, if any graphics display properly and the actual process of logging into your payment processing and then downloading your product. Not all mobile devices operate in the same way and people on IPad's oKen have a hard time opening zip files.

If you come across any type of issue, try to find a solution for it. Of course, if you run into an issue, no doubt many of your customer's will too. Just post your recommendations along with your instructions, or add them to a Frequently Asked Questions page.

CHAPTER 8

THE POPULARITY OF MOBILE MARKETING

If you take a look around you, you will no doubt see plenty of people using some type of mobile device. This might be a Smartphone, a laptop, eReader or IPad device. Just take a look and see how many people have some kind of mobile device, nowadays most people have at least one. This just goes to show you how important staying connected is.

People love to stay in contact with one another and mobile devices just make this so easy. You can now send text messages to say you are on your way home, or to remind your spouse to pick up dinner. Your children can text you when they will be home late from school. The convenience factor is huge.

Mobile devices really are a way for parents to stay connected with their children while they are out. This is actually a two way street as kids can text their parents if a situation arises and they suddenly need help. No more running off to find the nearest pay phone.

Even seniors are enjoying their mobile devices. This allows them to stay in contact with their family and helps them from feeling too lonely. A mobile device can help provide any person, young or old, with an added sense of security. You could even view a mobile device as a life line to the outside world.

You can see the popularity of mobile devices everywhere you go, and they can be used in different ways. You can add your grocery list to it, send yourself reminders, keep track of appointments and more.

Plus a mobile device can help you be more productive. While you are waiting for your doctor's appointment, you can check on your kids, update a report or check in with the office. Years ago you would just sit waiting idly for your appointment. A mobile device can really help you get the most out of each and every day.

It is very easy to stay connected with all your family, friends and your place of work. All you have to do is find a Wi- - Fi hot spot and you can easily connect to the internet. There is no reason why you can't always keep in touch with everyone, regardless of your location.

It really does pay to be a mobile user today. They allow you to keep in touch with your family at the touch of a button. Help or support will never be that far away again.

Final Words

Here are a few final tips to help you build stronger mobile marketing campaigns that will connect with your target audience:

Know Your Audience

In order to create mobile marketing campaigns that connect to your audience, you need to know *exactly* who they are.

For example, are they avid gamers? How old are they? Where do they spend most their time online? The more you know about your audience, the better you'll be able to create highly-targeted campaigns that generate results.

Try Different Mobile Marketing Strategies

Don't just stick to one mobile marketing campaign. Test out different types of mobile marketing to find out what works best for your business. Don't be afraid to branch out and try new things!

Test & Track Everything

Keep track of how your audience responds to different mobile marketing campaigns. That way you know where to invest your marketing dollars and what just isn't working.

Build an App for Your Ecommerce Site

Consider developing an app that highlights your products and caters to the mobile shopper. Incorporate a reward program into your marketing strategy that rewards loyal buyers.

Another area to look at when it comes to mobile devices is to see how your social sites display. These sites are accessed by your customers on a daily basis so ensuring they display correctly could help you increase your fan base.

If you haven't considered the aspect of mobile marketing it is time that you do just this.

9 786069 837153

Printed by Libri Plureos GmbH in Hamburg, Germany